CHAPTER ONE

"The Real People"

Centuries ago, a large Native American tribe lived in mountainous regions of what became the southeastern United States. They called themselves *Aniyunwiya,* meaning "the Real People," or "the Principal People." They are better known as the *Cherokee,* a name given to them by other Native Americans. This name may mean "Mountain People."

Before Europeans arrived, the Cherokee lived and hunted in what are now North and South Carolina, Georgia, Alabama, Tennessee, Virginia, West Virginia, and Kentucky. A typical Cherokee village had several hundred people. They hunted deer and elk, caught fish, and grew corn, beans, and squash. They built their homes

An example of a typical Cherokee home as it would have been built before the Europeans arrived.

with tree poles covered with bark, grass, and mud.

Cherokee children learned by working alongside adults and by listening to elders tell stories. According to one story, when the world was young, the Great Buzzard flew over the muddy land to explore it.

The Trail of Tears

The Trail of Tears

Dennis Brindell Fradin

Marshall Cavendish
Benchmark

Dedication

For my son, Anthony Derrick Fradin, with love

Marshall Cavendish Benchmark
99 White Plains Road
Tarrytown, New York 10591
www.marshallcavendish.us

Text and maps copyright © 2008 by Marshall Cavendish Corporation
Map on page 24 by Rodica Prato

All Internet sites were correct and accurate at time of printing.

Library of Congress Cataloging-in-Publication Data

Fradin, Dennis B.
The Trail of Tears / Dennis Brindell Fradin.
p. cm. — (Turning points in U.S. history)
Summary: "Covers the Trail of Tears as a watershed event in U.S. history, influencing social, economic, and political policies that shaped the nation's future"—Provided by publisher.
Includes bibliographical references and index.
ISBN-13: 978-0-7614-2041-5
1. Trail of Tears, 1838. 2. Cherokee Indians—Relocation. 3. Cherokee Indians—Government relations. 4. Cherokee Indians—Social conditions.
I. Title. II. Series.
E99.C5F685 2007
975.004'97557—dc22
2006025346

Photo research by Connie Gardner

Cover: An oil painting depicts the Cherokee people on the Trail of Tears after being removed from their land in 1838.
Title page: Cherokee-made clay beads on a fringed buckskin bag.

Cover photo by The Granger Collection
Title Page: NativeStock.com: Marilyn Angel Wynn
The photographs in this book are used by permission and through the courtesy of: *NativeStock.com:* Marilyn Angel Wynn, 6, 9, 16, 39; *Raymond Bial:* 8; *Corbis:* Blue Lantern Studio, 10; Kevin Flemming, 36; Peter Turnley, 38; *The Granger Collection:* 12, 23; *NorthWind Picture Archive:* 14, 12, 20, 32; *Art Resource:* National Portrait Gallery, Smithsonian Institution, 18; John Guthrie: 26.

Time Line: John Guthrie

Editor: Deborah Grahame
Publisher: Michelle Bisson
Art Director: Anahid Hamparian

Printed in Malaysia
1 3 5 6 4 2

Contents

This painted mural shows the people and dwellings of an ancient Cherokee village.

A turtle shell rattle with a deer hoof handle, used for ceremonies and events such as the Green Corn Dance.

He flew too low, and in some places his wings beat up ridges that became mountains. When the Cherokee people appeared, they settled in these mountainous regions.

Like other tribes, the Cherokee believed in numerous gods and spirits. When reddish lightning flashed through the mountains, they said it came from their thunder god *Asgaya Gigagei*, or "Red Man." Spirits called the Little People lived in mountain caves. These spirits usually remained invisible. They sometimes helped lost children.

The Cherokee held many religious ceremonies and dances. Each summer they held the Green Corn Dance to give thanks for the season's first corn. At the New Year's Dance in late November, each town put out its **sacred** fire that had burned all year. With the lighting of the new flame, people were supposed to forget old **grudges** and start fresh with everyone.

This 1920 book illustration shows Hernando de Soto encountering Native Americans at the Mississippi River.

CHAPTER TWO

Europeans Arrive

By the 1530s an estimated 25,000 Cherokee lived in sixty towns. Cherokee territory covered about 125,000 square miles (324,000 square kilometers). This is roughly the size of the state of New Mexico.

The first Europeans to encounter the Cherokee were Spaniards. Hernando de Soto, a Spanish explorer, came to North America seeking gold. He led an **expedition** through the American South from 1539 to 1542. The Cherokee provided the travelers with wild turkeys and corn to eat.

England began settling its American **colonies** in the early 1600s. English traders visited the Cherokee to exchange guns and other items for

Settlers brought deadly diseases, such as smallpox, to North America.

deerskins. The traders often moved into Cherokee towns. Some of them married Cherokee women.

Contact with Europeans brought **misery** to the Cherokee. Between the late 1600s and the early 1700s, thousands of Cherokee died of smallpox and other diseases spread by the Europeans. In addition, settlers fought several wars on North American soil in the 1700s. The Cherokee wanted to remain **neutral**, but they were pressured into taking one side or another.

When the Cherokee helped the losing side of a battle, they suffered at the hands of the winners. For example, in 1775 the American colonists **rebelled** against British rule. The Cherokee believed the British would squash the rebellion, so they agreed to help England. However, the colonists won their **independence**—and burned more than fifty Cherokee towns along the way.

The American Revolution ended in 1783. The Cherokee then had to deal with a new nation: the United States of America.

Covered wagons carried families westward across the plains during the 1800s.

CHAPTER THREE

"Never Again to Cede One Foot More of Land"

As American settlers moved steadily westward, new states were added to the original thirteen. By 1820 the United States had twenty-three states and about 10 million people.

Meanwhile, disease and warfare had taken their toll on the Cherokee. By the early 1800s the tribe's population was well below 20,000. This was below what it had been when the Cherokee had first encountered white people three centuries earlier.

American **pioneers** wanted Native American lands. They demanded that the tribes make **treaties** to trade land for food, money, and other items. Greatly outnumbered, the Native Americans had little choice.

Cherokee hunters used blowguns made of river cane.

As their hunting grounds grew smaller, they needed the food and other goods the treaties promised. After its twenty-fifth treaty with the settlers in 1819, the Cherokee Nation held only one-seventh of its original territory.

The Cherokee realized that they must act to survive as a people. Many of them decided to adopt some ways of white Americans. This, they believed, would convince the U.S. government to let them keep their remaining lands.

During the 1820s the Cherokee created a government like that of the United States. They established their capital at a Cherokee town

The title page of the constitution of the Cherokee Nation, established at New Echota, Georgia in 1827.

in Georgia and named it New Echota. The Cherokee government included a two-house legislature and a principal chief. This resembled the U.S. legislature and the president.

Another major event of the 1820s occurred when a Cherokee named Sequoyah devised a writing system for his people. The Cherokee opened schools where children learned to read and write in both their own language and English. The Cherokee established a printing press at New Echota. They published books and, starting in 1828, a newspaper called the *Cherokee Phoenix*.

Sequoyah

Sequoyah is believed to have been born at a Cherokee village in Tennessee. Sequoyah became a silversmith, but his dream was to create a written Cherokee language. In 1821, after twelve years of work, he completed a Cherokee writing system consisting of about eighty-five symbols. Sequoyah taught his system to his daughter Ayoka, and together they demonstrated it. The Cherokee soon adopted Sequoyah's alphabet. The man who made it possible for the Cherokee to read and write in their own language later settled in Oklahoma.

Sequoyah (1770?–1843)

Many Cherokee became Christians. Some built large estates where black slaves grew their crops. But the Cherokees vowed to oppose the whites on one issue. At a meeting at New Echota in 1823, they declared, "It is the determination of this Nation never again to **cede** one foot more of land." Cherokee who sold tribal lands without their government's consent would be condemned to death.

Prospectors came to Cherokee land in Georgia during the early 1800s to pan the streams for gold.

CHAPTER FOUR

"We Wish to Remain on the Land of Our Fathers"

The Cherokee's hopes of being left in peace were shattered in 1829. That summer, gold was found on Cherokee land in northern Georgia. The Cherokee were powerless to stop the gold rush that followed. A town named Dahlonega (from a Cherokee word meaning "golden") grew up at the site of the gold-mining camps.

The white **intruders** saw that the Cherokee Nation had rich farmland and valuable timber in addition to gold. They wanted the Cherokee territory. President Andrew Jackson agreed that the Cherokee must move to make way for the settlers. On May 28, 1830, Jackson signed the Indian Removal Act. It allowed the U.S. government to pressure Native Americans to leave existing states.

The federal and state governments tried to force the Cherokee to make a land exchange and move beyond the Mississippi River. The state of Georgia decided to treat the Cherokee so badly that they would want to leave. Under Georgia law, some Cherokee were arrested—or even shot—for mining gold on their own land.

Led by Principal Chief John Ross, the Cherokee waged a nearly ten-year struggle to keep their homelands. They fought in court and wrote to lawmakers. On July 17, 1830, the Cherokee issued an appeal: "We wish to remain on the land of our fathers . . . the land which gave us birth."

Nearly all Cherokee agreed with Chief Ross that they must never give up their remaining tribal lands. However, a small number of Cherokee thought it best to exchange tribal lands for western territory. This group was called the Treaty Party. Its leaders included a Cherokee lawmaker known as The Ridge, his son John, and Elias Boudinot, former editor of the *Cherokee Phoenix.*

The U.S. government did something sneaky. While Chief Ross was on a trip to Washington, D.C., U.S. officials met with about two hundred Treaty Party members at New Echota. Even though they represented a small **minority** of Cherokee, Treaty Party leaders signed an agreement in December 1835. According to the Treaty of New Echota, the Cherokee agreed to "**relinquish** to the United States

John Ross (Kooweskoowe)

Kooweskoowe, meaning "The Egret," was thought to have been born in Alabama. He is better known by his English name, John Ross. Ross had both Scottish and Cherokee ancestry, and he was highly educated.

Around 1815 he founded a trading post that grew into the city of Chattanooga, Tennessee. In the 1820s he helped draft the Cherokee Constitution, and in 1828 he was elected principal chief.

Chief Ross led a brave struggle to hold on to his people's lands. He suffered personal tragedy on the Trail of Tears when his wife Quatie died on the journey. Still principal chief after nearly forty years, Ross died in Washington, D.C., while on business for his people, at the age of seventy-five.

John Ross (1790–1866)

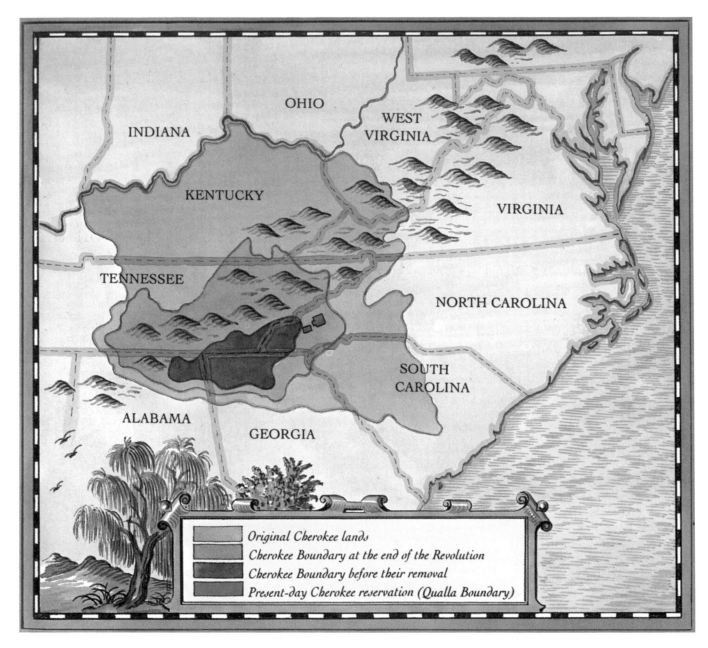

This map shows how the Cherokee homelands grew smaller over time, as the U.S. government seized more territory.

all the lands possessed by them east of the Mississippi River." In exchange the Cherokee would receive 5 million dollars and "new homes" in the West.

Upon learning what had occurred, Chief Ross and most of the Cherokee were enraged. A small number of Cherokee had agreed to sell tribal lands against the will of the **majority**. On May 23, 1836, by a single vote, the U.S. Senate ruled that the Treaty of New Echota must be obeyed. Within two years, the Cherokee would have to move off their homelands in the South and settle in what is now Oklahoma.

A modern painting depicts the Cherokee enduring the harsh winter as they traveled the Trail of Tears.

The Trail of Tears

By late 1836 more than six thousand Cherokee had moved westward. Nearly 20,000 others were determined to stay until they were forced out. As a last-ditch effort, Chief Ross presented a **petition** to the U.S. Congress in early 1838. It contained 15,000 signatures—which amounted to most of the Cherokee tribe—protesting the Treaty of New Echota. "What is our crime?" the petition asked. "Are we to be hunted through the mountains, like wild beasts, and our women, our children, our aged, our sick, to be dragged from their homes?"

Sadly, the answer was yes.

The government rejected the petition. Martin Van Buren, now

White People Against the Trail of Tears

Many white people opposed the U.S. policy of forcing Native Americans from their lands. U.S. Senator Theodore Frelinghuysen of New Jersey was strongly against the Indian Removal Act. In a speech before the U.S. Senate in April 1830, Frelinghuysen called the plan to move the Cherokee an "evil hour" in U.S. history. Famed frontiersman Davy Crockett, representing Tennessee in the House of Representatives, told his fellow Congressmen in May 1830 that the Indian Removal Act was so unfair he would vote against it even if he were "the only man in the United States who disapproved it." Author Ralph Waldo Emerson also criticized the treatment of the Cherokee. In a letter to President Martin Van Buren in 1838, Emerson declared that if the U.S. tried "to hold the [Cherokee] to this **sham** treaty . . . the name of this nation . . . will stink to the world."

president of the United States, assigned General Winfield Scott the job of forcing the Cherokee to leave. General Scott and his seven thousand soldiers arrived at New Echota in May 1838.

About 1,400 Cherokee, most of them in North Carolina, escaped removal. They either hid from the soldiers or were allowed to stay in their homes on land that they owned privately. In May and June of 1838, the remaining Cherokee—about 17,000 people—were rounded up along with their two thousand slaves. They were placed in **stockades** that resembled prison camps. John Burnett, a soldier who took part in the removal, later wrote,

*Men working in the fields were arrested and driven to the stockades. Women were dragged from their homes by soldiers. Children were often separated from their parents and driven into the stockades. And often the old and **infirm** were prodded with bayonets to hasten them to the stockades.*

Cherokee who tried to flee from the stockades were brutally whipped. From the stockades the Cherokee and their slaves were led to three places, two in Tennessee and one in Alabama. From there, they would make the trip to Oklahoma. Between June and December of 1838, the Cherokee and their slaves set out in about sixteen groups. Although some people made the one-thousand-mile (sixteen-hundred-kilometer) journey by boat or horse and wagon, most traveled on foot.

The trip to Oklahoma took about half a year, including the winter months. Along the way, the travelers suffered from cold and **fatigue**. Weakened by the hardships of the trip, many fell ill and died. Others

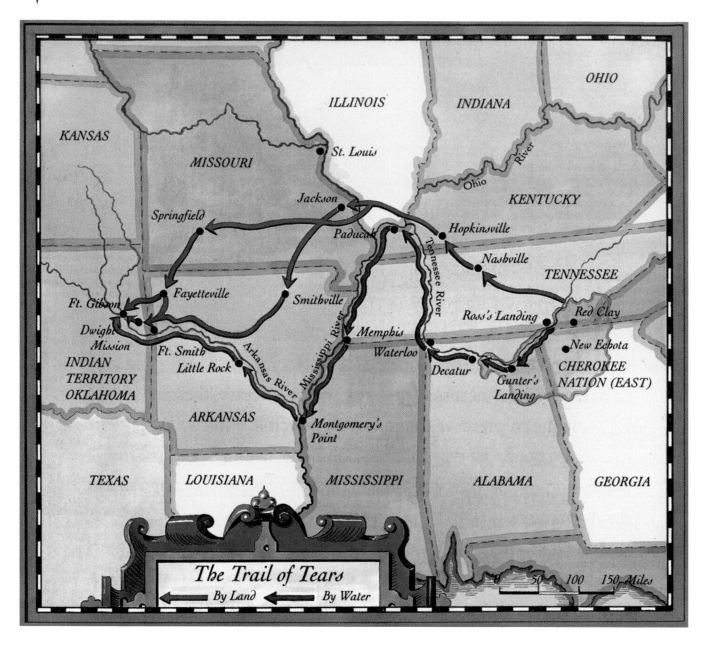

The Trail of Tears

← By Land ← By Water

This map shows the Trail of Tears routes taken by land and by water.

starved to death. Some collapsed in the snow and could go no farther. An unidentified Cherokee later recalled,

> *Women cry and make sad wails. Children cry and*
> *many men cry, and all look sad when friends die,*
> *but they say nothing and just put heads down*
> *and keep on go towards west. People die very*
> *much but always we keep marching on.*

The Cherokee stopped only to rest briefly and to bury their dead. Because so many of their people died on the way to Oklahoma, in time the Cherokee called the journey *Nunna daul Isunyi*, or "The Trail Where We Cried." In English it became known as the Trail of Tears. Approximately four thousand Cherokee and several hundred of their slaves died during the roundup, the imprisonment, or on the Trail of Tears to Oklahoma.

Other Native American groups also braved cruel conditions when they were forced from their lands.

CHAPTER SIX

After the Trail of Tears:

More Tears

The Trail of Tears was a turning point in relations between the United States and Native Americans. The Cherokee way of life resembled that of white Americans, so it seemed to be the least likely tribe to be forced to move. But that had happened. It sent a message across North America: When settlers wanted Indian lands, the United States would find a way to remove the Native Americans. Over the next few decades, many other tribes were forced off their homelands, often after U.S. soldiers defeated them in battle.

The Trail of Tears was also a landmark event in Cherokee history. Thousands of people died on the journey, and the survivors continued to

Defining the Trail of Tears

The term *Trail of Tears* usually refers to the Cherokee's trip to Oklahoma. However, other Southeastern tribes also were driven out of their homes to lands farther west. Between 1830 and 1842, Choctaw, Chickasaw, Creek, and Seminole Indians were pushed from their homelands and forced to resettle in Oklahoma. Their trips resulted in misery and death and so the removal of each of these tribes is also called "the Trail of Tears."

face hardships in Oklahoma. In June 1839 groups of Cherokee men killed Treaty Party leaders: The Ridge, his son John Ridge, and Elias Boudinot. This was widely seen as a fair punishment for their role in the Treaty of New Echota. However, it sparked several years of fighting between the Treaty Party and other Cherokee. Not until the mid-1840s did the two sides agree to live in peace.

More trouble came during the Civil War (1861–1865). The Union, or North, fought the Confederacy, or South, largely over slavery. The Cherokee still owned slaves, and Oklahoma was in the country's southern part, so many members of the tribe sided with the Confederacy. The Union won the war, and the Cherokee, like other Southerners, had to free their slaves. As punishment for siding with

Gallegina

Gallegina, known in English as Elias Boudinot (1800–1839), was born in Georgia. The oldest of nine children, he attended one of the Christian schools that missionaries established in the Cherokee Nation in the early 1800s. Boudinot became editor of the *Cherokee Phoenix*, the first newspaper published by Native Americans.

At first Boudinot agreed with Chief Ross that the Cherokee should not make a treaty to sell their lands. Later, he concluded that the Cherokee had no choice but to move. He and other Treaty Party leaders signed the Treaty of New Echota at the Boudinot home in late 1835. For their role in giving up Cherokee land, Elias Boudinot, his uncle The Ridge, and his cousin John Ridge were attacked and killed. This took place on June 22, 1839, soon after their people completed the Trail of Tears to Oklahoma.

the South, the Cherokee had more lands taken from them in 1866.

In the late 1800s the U.S. government struck again at the Cherokee and other Native Americans. Their tribal lands were broken up and distributed to individual Native American families. Tribal governments also were ended. These acts were intended to abolish, or end, tribal rule in Oklahoma and to prepare the territory for statehood. Oklahoma officially became a state in 1907.

Members of the Cherokee Nation still celebrate traditional dances at festivals.

CHAPTER SEVEN

The Cherokee Rise Again

The Cherokee revived their tribal identity in the 1900s. They re-established their tribal government at the Cherokee capital of Tahlequah, Oklahoma. The *Cherokee Phoenix* was brought back to life. New tribal **constitutions** were adopted in 1976 and 2003.

The Cherokee also established schools, health clinics, and many kinds of businesses, from real estate to gambling casinos. At the same time they have kept alive old customs, such as traditional dances, storytelling, and their language.

Today, the Cherokee is one of the country's largest Indian tribes. More than 250,000 Native Americans belong to the Cherokee Nation in

Wilma Mankiller

Wilma Mankiller

One of eleven children, Wilma Mankiller was born in Tahlequah, Oklahoma, in 1945. "I experienced my own Trail of Tears," she once wrote, recalling the hardships she had to overcome. As Wilma was growing up, her poverty-stricken family lacked indoor plumbing and heating. Later, Wilma was seriously injured in a car wreck. But she survived, and dedicated her life to her people.

In 1985 she became the Cherokee Nation's first female principal chief, and served in that role for ten years. During that time she oversaw the construction of schools and health clinics, and helped her people open businesses. Wilma Mankiller is considered one of the great leaders in Cherokee history.

The seal of the Cherokee Nation is displayed at the entrance of the tribal building in Cherokee, North Carolina.

Oklahoma. More than ten thousand others comprise the Eastern Band of Cherokee Indians in North Carolina. In addition, thousands of Cherokee live scattered across the country.

The Cherokee have shed many tears and suffered hard times. But they have also shown the world how to survive as a people.

Glossary

cede—To give up or hand over.

colonies—Settlements built by a country outside of its borders.

constitutions—Basic frameworks of government.

expedition—A journey or trip.

fatigue—The state of being very tired.

grudges—Feelings of anger or ill will that last a long time.

independence—Freedom or self-government.

infirm—Weak, often as a result of old age.

intruders—People who have entered without permission.

majority—An amount more than half of the total number.

minority—An amount less than half of the total number.

misery—Great unhappiness or suffering.

neutral—Not taking a side in a dispute or war.

petition—A written request often including a list of signed names.

pioneers—The first people to explore and settle a new territory.

rebelled—Disobeyed or protested.

relinquish—To give up or hand over.

sacred—Holy; important in a religious way.

sham—Fake.

stockades—Fortresses built to lock people in or to keep people out.

treaties—Formal agreements, often written, between two or more groups.

Timeline

1539–1542—Hernando de Soto leads a Spanish expedition for gold through the American South, providing the Cherokee with their first known encounter with Europeans

1761—The British destroy fifteen Cherokee towns to punish them for aiding the French in the French and Indian War

1775–1783—The American Revolution results in the birth of the United States; the Cherokee take the British side in the war and have fifty of their towns burned by the Americans

1785—The Treaty of Hopewell, the first treaty between the United States and the Cherokee tribe, is made at Hopewell, South Carolina

1821—Sequoyah completes his Cherokee writing system

1827—The Cherokee create a constitution establishing a government similar to that of the United States

1828—The *Cherokee Phoenix* is first issued

1829—Gold is found on Cherokee land in northern Georgia

1761   *1785*   *1821*

1830—President Andrew Jackson signs the Indian Removal Act, allowing the U.S. government to pressure Native Americans to leave existing states

1835—Treaty Party leaders sign the Treaty of New Echota, by which they cede Cherokee homelands and agree that the tribe will move to Oklahoma

1838–1839—Most Cherokee are sent to Oklahoma along the Trail of Tears; about four thousand Cherokee and several hundred of their slaves die in the removal from their homes or on the journey

1900s—Cherokee revive the *Cherokee Phoenix*, establish businesses, create a new tribal constitution, choose the first female principal chief, and achieve a great deal in many fields

1988–1989—150th anniversary of the tragic Cherokee Trail of Tears

2003—The Cherokee adopt a new constitution

2007—Oklahoma celebrates one hundred years of statehood; the Cherokee, with 250,000 members in the Cherokee Nation in Oklahoma and thousands of people elsewhere, are one of the country's largest Indian tribes

1838–1839   *2003*

Further Information

BOOKS

Birchfield, D. L. *The Trail of Tears*. Milwaukee, WI: World Almanac Library, 2004.

De Capua, Sarah. *The Cherokee*. New York: Marshall Cavendish, 2006.

Dennis, Yvonne Wakim. *Sequoyah: 1770?–1843*. Mankato, MN: Blue Earth Books, 2004.

Elish, Dan. *The Trail of Tears: The Story of the Cherokee Removal*. New York: Marshall Cavendish, 2002.

Fischer, Laura. *Life on the Trail of Tears*. Chicago: Heinemann, 2003.

Fitterer, C. Ann. *Sequoyah: Native American Scholar*. Chanhassen, MN: The Child's World, 2003.

WEB SITES

Official Web sites of tribes involved in the Removal
www.cherokee.org
www.chickasaw.net
www.choctawnation.com
www.muscogeenation-nsn.gov
www.seminolenation.com

A fact sheet for young people about the Cherokee, with links to many
related sites
www.geocities.com/bigorrin/cherokee_kids.htm

An engaging description of the Trail of Tears
NationalTOTA.org

Home page for information about Sequoyah from the Sequoyah
Birthplace Museum
www.sequoyahmuseum.org/

Bibliography

Anderson, William L., ed. *Cherokee Removal: Before and After*. Athens: University of Georgia Press, 1991.

Carter, Samuel III. *Cherokee Sunset: A Nation Betrayed*. Garden City, New York: Doubleday, 1976.

Filler, Louis, and Allen Guttmann, eds. *The Removal of the Cherokee Nation: Manifest Destiny or National Dishonor?* Boston: Heath, 1962.

King, Duane H., ed. *The Cherokee Indian Nation: A Troubled History*. Knoxville: University of Tennessee Press, 1979.

Long, Cathryn J. *The Cherokee*. San Diego: Lucent, 2000.

Perdue, Theda, and Michael D. Green, eds. *The Cherokee Removal: A Brief History with Documents*. Boston: Bedford Books of St. Martin's Press, 1995.

Index

Page numbers in **boldface** are illustrations.

About the Author

Dennis Fradin is the author of 150 books, some of them written with his wife, Judith Bloom Fradin. Their recent book for Clarion, *The Power of One: Daisy Bates and the Little Rock Nine*, was named a Golden Kite Honor Book. Another of Dennis's recent books is *Let It Begin Here! Lexington & Concord: First Battles of the American Revolution*, published by Walker. The Fradins are currently writing a biography of social worker and antiwar activist Jane Addams for Clarion and a nonfiction book about a slave escape for National Geographic Children's Books. Turning Points in U.S. History is Dennis Fradin's first series for Marshall Cavendish Benchmark. The Fradins have three grown children and three young grandchildren.